Singer of Seasons

We are facing the future
ready to begin again,
ready to believe in ourselves again,
our marriages,
our lives,

ready to try to trust you one more time.
O singer of seasons,
see us through.

D1293811

SINGER OF SEASONS

THE PRAYERS OF BEVERLY SAWYER

With a Foreword by
Dr. James Argue

Illustrations by
Madeline Collins

August House/Little Rock

Publishers

© 1982 by Beverly Sawyer.
© 1990 by Emma Lee Sawyer.
All rights reserved. This book, or parts thereof,
may not be reproduced in any form without permission.
Published by August House, Inc.,
P.O. Box 3223, Little Rock, Arkansas, 72203.
501-372-5450.

Printed in the United States of America

10 9 8 7 6 5 4 3

ISBN 0-935304-42-8

Library of Congress Card Number 82-70161
Sawyer, Beverly:
Singer of seasons: Prayers
Little Rock: August House
100 pp., original paperback

FOREWORD

I have a feeling that congregations seldom look forward with anticipation and excitement to the pastoral prayer in Sunday morning worship. This is decidedly *not* the case, however, at Pulaski Heights United Methodist Church on those Sundays when Beverly Sawyer is serving as liturgist. On those days, when Beverly steps to the lectern, one senses that the congregation is truly preparing for encounter with the Almighty. As the prayer is offered, it becomes far more than Beverly's prayer. It becomes the prayer of all, as each worshipper achieves indentification with phrase after phrase.

I have tried to analyze Beverly's unique ability in this area. How can one — especially one so young — have such a profound understanding of the human condition? Part of it comes from her sensitivity, a sensitivity so acute that she easily identifies with the significant joys and deep hurts of young and old, male and female, married and single. Her great interest in literature undoubtedly provides help in word selection and other aspects of the creative process. Her concern for the downtrodden and oppressed lends a passion and a relevance to her prayers. Her faith is the force that focuses all of her many skills and abilities in the service of God and His people.

Whatever the formula for her prayer ability, these prayers are beautiful devotional experiences. I am happy that this volume will provide the wider distribution that they deserve.

James B. Argue
Senior Minister
Pulaski Heights United Methodist Church
Little Rock, Arkansas

January, 1982

SPRING

Almost every morning this week
we've wakened to the sound of rain,
and then somewhere,
half-way between
brushing teeth
and brushing hair,
50,000 rain-drenched birds
started singing
the "Hallelujah Chorus"
out in the yard.

We had to smile
in spite of ourselves.

We had to smile,
for whatever is happening
to this winter-worn world
is happening to us too.

Some dormant capacity for hope,
that we thought had died long ago
is stirring and waking
within us —
some ability to believe,
is mysteriously reviving itself,
and we find that all the old worry,
and old joy,
that we thought we had
filed away like photographs
have been just below
the frozen surface
all along.

It's a kind of being reborn
and we don't understand it a bit —
how when we have every reason
to be discouraged,
disillusioned,
and despairing,
we find we are as
lighthearted as those silly birds.

Those silly birds
have hovered all night
somewhere trying to stay out of the rain.
They've been blown about by the wind,
shaken by the thunder,
drenched by the downpour,
and now in the dawn
they are turning
the storm into song.

We smile because we know
we really are like them —
we've hovered
through our own human storms
and we've been blown about
and drenched,
and yet here we are
trying to turn storm
into song.

Support us in our search
O God almighty, like a father.
Comfort us in our struggle,
O God eternal,
like a mother.

Creator of life,
give us new life.
Maker of bird song,
help us sing.

Amen.

It's April already.
Another winter is over.
Another basketball season is gone.

We're a year older all right;
last year's shorts don't fit,
and we've never had to use Ben Gay before
at least not after mowing the yard.

We're a year older all right;
we looked up from the newspaper
this morning to realize
our son must have grown six inches this year,
and our daughters are talking about
the University and Hendrix
and Ronnie what's-his-name.

We're a year older all right;
We started getting social security checks
and pictures of grandkids in the mail,
or
we got the braces off our teeth
and the opposite sex is beginning to
notice we exist.

Forgive us for being too tired
to do the things we enjoy.

Forgive us for being lonely
because we're too proud
to reach out

Forgive us for not stopping
to say "I love you"
to you and to one another.

Forgive us for not saying
"Thank you".

Forgive us for ~~being so~~
~~busy we forget to pray.~~
not taking time to pray.
AMEN

We can't even remember
what we did all year.
Now it just seems like a blur
of classes and carpools,
of mornings and meetings,
trips to the doctor
and arguments about who gets the car.

Forgive us God,
for being so busy we didn't notice
the year go by.
Forgive us for taking ourselves so seriously,
that we went back down to the office,
instead of sharing our lives
with one another.

Forgive us for always being too tired
to do the things we enjoy.
Forgive us for being lonely
because we're too proud
to reach out.

Forgive us for not stopping to say
"I love you"
to you and to one another.
Forgive us for not saying "Thank you."

Frankly God,
we forgot that it was Mothers' Day,
until we bumped into
Mrs. So-in-So
at the store.
What a rush — but we got the flowers
and the card okay,
and the dinner is going to come off
if nothing unexpected happens.

Now,
as for Pentecost,
which we are also celebrating here today:
We didn't forget,
we just didn't know about it at all.
Or at least we didn't
know when,
and we haven't really been very curious
about it.

So we are celebrating
all kinds of things today,
but mostly we are
worried about the roast . . .
and whether or not
we can successfully spend
the afternoon with our in-laws.

We are reluctant celebrants, God.
It seems like we drag our feet
and gripe,
we mumble
and hesitate,
on every occasion.

If everyone else
sings really loudly,
we might join in . . .
if we're sure no one will hear us.

Celebrating is risky
because it is an admission that
we care,
and that we invest ourselves . . .
and we're afraid of being disappointed.
If everyone else sings really loudly
it would be easier.

If everyone else really enjoyed themselves
and kind of got caught up in
the spirit of things —
if you'd just send your spirit, God,
your powerful
and overwhelming presence,
it would be easier.

And then we realize
you already have:

That when we love each other
you are there;
when we support each other
that is your sustaining presence;
when we comfort each other;
and when we laugh;
when we share a cup of coffee,
or a dream;
when we greet each other;
and when we say good-bye;
in our everyday acts of community
your spirit is there
in a powerful and overwhelming way.
When we are together
we *are* celebrating . . .
even if we don't sing loudly.

We realize that when we begin
to understand ourselves
as brothers and sisters,
we begin to truly be the family of God:
when we understand our mutual dependency
on one another
and on you,
we truly become the children of God . . .

and Pentecost,
the celebration of your spirit,
and Mothers' Day,
the celebration of family love
strangely become
in fact
the same celebration.

Happy Mothers' Day, God.

Love,
Your Kids.

We imagine
that the procession was great,
God — was it?
We imagine the streets packed
with onlookers
in a holiday mood,
brought together by the news
that the king
was coming into town.
Someone was passing out palms,
and shouting instructions
down the line.
Someone was selling a snack.
A baby was crying.

They had waited for the king,
not just that day,
but all their lives.

They had waited
for the king to come
and save them from the Romans,
and save them from famine,
and save them from war.
They had waited for the
king to come,
and solve all their problems
and fill all their needs
and answer all their prayers.

We imagine that the cheer
went up,
and *Hosanna* rang through the streets
like something from Handel —
that the palms
went down,
row upon row upon row,
and you rode
serenely into town
on that borrowed colt.

Was it like that?

Or was it instead like some
scene from our own lives,
some ordinary daily scene;
like the havoc
before the school bus arrives,
or the last minute dash
for Easter clothes?
Was it perhaps like the stillness
in the house
after a funeral,
or the stillness
in the heart after the divorce?

a hospital waiting room?
an empty and lonely kitchen?
an office fraught with tension?
a traffic jam on Cantrell?
or an airport ticket line?

Did they organize
a "Jerusalem Hosanna Choir,"
rehearsing in advance
for the triumphant entry?

Or did they just look up one
day as we might,
and see you coming
around the corner of their lives,
and whisper
out of astonished desperation
as we would?
"Hosanna —
Save us now."

The new shoes
were too tight.
The new dress was too itchy,
and fifteen minutes before
leaving for church,
someone got sick on chocolate eggs.
O God,
Easter
has almost become the production
that Christmas is,
but
here in the pew
quiet for a moment,
we can breathe a sigh of relief.
The in-laws are coming for lunch,
but that's an hour or so away —
one hour left before the next
festive onslaught.

Here in the pew
we have an hour,
to think, to listen,
to sing, to pray.
What should we pray for, God?
What is a proper prayer
this chocolate-egg
and Lily day,
this first Sunday,
this holy day?

Should we thank you
that you pushed
the stone away
and left the grave
proving you were in fact
God on earth,
by performing a miracle
that topped them all?
Should we be mystified by your passion,
the gift of your death,
the miracle of your resurrection?

We pray those prayers dutifully,
but we confess we are distracted
by the shoes that pinch our feet,
and the upcoming family meal.
Perhaps we should
thank you instead,
that the sun came up this morning,
that the birds woke and sang,
that the coffeepot perked
and pushed its wake-up smell
throughout the house.
Perhaps we should be mystified
by the beauty of clean towels
and the miracle of hot showers,
by a sleepy kiss
from a grumpy spouse
and the washer and dryer
which made clean socks possible.
Perhaps we should pray
for hope in its household form,
and for new life
in Little Rock.

Overcome for us, O God,
the death of everyday vitality,
make the miracle again
for us —
here —
Give us back the laughter,
the enthusiasm,
the optimism,
the dreams,
that have been deadened by dull reality.
Roll the stone away from our cold
hearts and make us love
and live again.

Amen.

We woke today, O God
to the sound of ~~trains,~~ *a plane*
and smiled, perhaps because
it seems that in ~~Pine Bluff~~ *Little Rock*
there is always
~~a train hissing and whining~~ *A plane thundering*
in the distance —
going somewhere.

We woke today with the hope
that today would be as splendid
as yesterday,
with plans of picnics,
or playgrounds,
or painting.

We woke up a little sore
from yesterday's yard work,
a little hoarse from football-shouting,
but feeling nevertheless
newly created and free.
We rubbed our eyes,
dizzy from our dreams,
and looked in the mirror
and remembered.
We remembered pain;

the sudden phone call
on an ordinary day,
when a stunned voice on the other end
announces death;

the fear of illness,
and the silent hours
in the plastic chairs of waiting rooms
as nurses and aides pass briskly by,
saved from our fear
by their busyness;

the terror of conflict,
shouting,
tense and angry voices,
cruel words;

the vastness of loneliness,
of houses with rooms
emptied of their laughter by time,
speaking their hollow creaking
through listless days,
and interminable nights.
We remembered pain this morning, God —
our dread of it —
our helplessness before it —
and are baffled
that on these beautiful September days
hearts break, and death intrudes.

Do not leave us alone, God, in our pain,
or in our awareness of the pain of others.
Stay near us,
and brood over us with your simple love.
Give us the comfort of your presence,
and the refuge of your name.
Embrace us with the tears
of those who cry with us,
and comfort us
with the Kleenex and coffee,
offered by puzzled but loving friends.
Give us,
if not understanding, courage —
and if not courage, endurance.

Wake us each morning
with the sound of trains,
with smiles at simple daily joys
and send us, filled with hope,
into the painful world.

Amen.

We thank you,
O God,
for tears of true regret,

for the futile wish
that words
had not been said,

for the chagrined hope
that all
could be forgotten.

We thank you
for the moments
when we do not like ourselves,
when the shadowy person
that we do not wish to be
lives out our most ignoble fears.

We thank you
for humble moments
of self-embarrassment,
for the flare
of temper
and sudden words.

We thank you
for guilt,
the quiet voice
that knows our imperfections
and, in our most
pompous moments,
calls us to remember
who we are.

We thank you
for failure,
and for broken dreams
which have cost us grief
but made us tolerant
and compassionate
with others.

For all these things
we strongly give you thanks,
for they
are but the painful prelude
to grace.
For grace, O God,
we praise you.

Grace,
by all its names:
the birth of each day's waking,
the green
and re-green of trees,
the smile of a spouse,
the laughter of friends,
the handshake of a colleague.

For your limitless *yes*
to who
we can be
and yet never are,
we give you thanks.

Amen.

Most mornings, God,
we wake with the alarm;
a quick shower,
a glance at the headlines,
a quick kiss and we're off,

to the office,
or the classroom,
to the kitchen,
or the carpool,
to whatever tasks call us into the day.

Usually we wake
with the day
already upon us,
and yawns and gulped cups of coffee
are just part of the routine.

This morning
we were awakened
by a disturbance in the yard,
a racket on the roof —
a gutter-glutting rain.

We hung for a moment
between daylight and dream,
and then the birds began.
They were determined to sing;
whether it was in spite of the rain,
or because of the rain,
we, who are ignorant of their language,
couldn't tell.
But they were still
fully in chorus
when the rain slacked into a sprinkle.

Then someone stirred in the house,
feet hit the floor
and the people we know best
began yawning
and gargling.

O God Almighty,
before we came to church this morning
we were in your sanctuary
and we listened to the Sabbath sounds
of a day being born.

We forget sometimes
in the cubicles of cars,
and offices,
elevators and corridors
that the world is even there,
and in our struggle to be accepted,
and applauded,
we forget we share the stage
with birds
and rainstorms,
with dawn
and every waking creature
you've brought into your day.

Giver of Life,
we loved you this morning
when we were most ourselves —
drowsy and innocent,
dressed only in our dreams.

We worshipped you with the wonder
of seeing anew
things we have long taken for granted

and we meant
when we first
said it this day,

Good morning.

They've filled Fort Chaffee
with refugees, God,
Cubans,
speaking Spanish,
saying things we cannot understand
about places we've never seen.

We pick up the newspapers
and we don't know how to feel,
as Klansmen
march in the same old sheets,
spreading the same old hate
out of the same old fear.

We pick up the newspapers,
and we don't know how to feel.
We're not about
to don a sheet.
We don't hate these unknown
men and women,
and their sultry speech.
We don't hate
their desperate quest
for a more tolerable life.
We don't even hate
the Klansmen,
proud of their ignoble costumes,
reviving the bigotry
of their grandparents,
seasoned with smug superiority.

We do not hate,
but we are afraid —
afraid of such an influx of people,
wide-eyed
and Spanish tongued.

Where will they live?
And where will they work?
How will their children go to school?
Won't they be resented by the poor?
And how will other racial groups
respond,
as yet another group tries to melt into
the pot?

How will we ever understand
the babel of their speech —
the words
that divide us?

Come, Holy Spirit,
on this Pentecost day
and work the miracle of Pentecost again.

Make our mouths speak with truth.
Make our ears hear with love.
And make our hearts understand
that people are divided
by hate and fear,
not by speech,
        or culture,
        or ideology,
        or economy.

Give us the gift of tongues —
not to babble ecstatic prayer,
but to speak words of reconciliation
and hope.

Amen.

We pray, O God,
this morning
for the nameless faces in daily crowds;
for the man standing next to us in
the elevator,
for the cleaning woman
we pass in the hall,
for the new neighbors next door
who hurry and shout
and do not speak,
for the hitchhikers,
we pass in the rain — all bearded, all dirty
most young —
who are bound for some
indefinite destination.

We pray, O God, this morning
for the faceless names
in the daily paper;
for the woman
arrested for her husband's death,
for the man
who was killed driving home from work,
for the firemen who are striking,
and the railroad workers
who have lost their jobs,
and seen an era end.

We pray for those, O God,
involved in the banal and
the bizarre events of everyday life,
those whom we pity
and those whom we disdain,
those whom we envy
and those whom we admire.

We pray for these people, God,
for we too
are the faces and names of which
crowds are composed,
we pass people in corridors,
or in a traffic jam,
or in the grocery store,
and are never seen again.

We are the people
the neighbors don't know,
our co-workers don't know,
whose names appear
in the newspaper:
     Survivors are:
     Divorce filed by:
     Baby born to:
We are the lonely,
the grief-stricken,
the frightened,
the angry,
the frustrated.

We are the modern-day version
of that Jewish peasant crowd
who looked up one day
to see the answer to their prayers
clopping into town.
We are the ones, who, like they,
have made our niche in history
by saying "Yes" —
"Blessed is he who comes in the name of
the Lord."

We pray, O God
this morning
that there is a palm for us,
that we may have the courage
to add our face to the crowd
and our *hosanna* to the song.

Palm Sunday
    1980

God
today some of us are experiencing sorrow
from the death of
a family member,
or a marriage,
or a dream.

WHAT HAPPENS, LET ALL OF IT BE A BLESSING TO YOU.

Some of us are uncertain
about our work,
and the worth of our labor;
we're re-evaluating
and facing the emptiness of tasks that
have become mechanical.

WHAT HAPPENS, LET ALL OF IT BE A BLESSING TO YOU.

Some of us confront
the pain and ambiguity of illness,
hospitalization,
medication and
limitation.

WHAT HAPPENS, LET ALL OF IT BE A BLESSING TO YOU.

Some of us are lonely
in our empty
or crowded lives.
We seek for bridges into other human hearts.

But all of us —
those who grieve,
and those who are uncertain,
those who suffer illness,
and those who are alone —
seek to embrace our experiences,
befriend the world,
and love our lives.

Help us to accept our grief
as pain
that will empower us to live;
our uncertainty
as a difficult opportunity
to discover unknown
dreams and directions;
our illnesses
as a strong light
which helps us see at last
our health;
our loneliness
as the most authentic beginning
of human love
and solidarity.

Help us,
not to be pollyanna pieties
but
sincere seekers
for wholeness of life.
Help us to open the door of the
morning and say:

WHAT HAPPENS, LET ALL OF IT BE A BLESSING.

Amen.

SUMMER

For simple summer mornings, God,
we give you thanks:
for the silence exchanged
between men and women,
and the laughter shared
by boys and girls,

for the lazy sound
of the coffee perking,
and the newspaper
tightly curled
and tempting,

for the patches of sun
peeking through trees,
and the neighbor's radio
distant
and droning.

For simple summer mornings, God,
we give you thanks:
for the moment
or half-moment
of waking,
when for an instant we hover
and stare at our own world,
strangers,
before we remember who we are;

for the moment of remembering
and all its
accompanying joy and sorrow;

for the delight
of finding oneself once again
embodied,
and the grief
of rediscovering finitude.

For simple summer mornings, God,
we give you thanks:
for toes bare and wiggling,
and tile floors cool to toes,
for shoes to take toes walking,
and for hands tieing shoes,
and teeth and hands
brushing,
for all motion
and combinations
of moving.

For simple summer mornings, God,
we give you thanks:
for places to go
and people waiting there for us,
for conversations
we will share,
and hellos
and how-are-you's,
that we will say and really mean;

for the day
filled with human comments
yet to come,
and the hours that will lumber
humidly toward night
and sleep.

For simple summer mornings, God,
we give you thanks.

Amen.

We come today, O Lord
from our Summer lives;
from the patios, pools, and playgrounds
of our leisure.
We come sunburned and bug-bitten —
the victors
of a hard-fought baseball game,
or swim meet,
or tennis match.
We come having dressed out of the
confusion of our suitcases,
which are being packed
or
unpacked,
or
packed again.
We come
out of a myriad of plans,
dates, deadlines,
trips and tournaments.
We are busy people
when we play.

But we do not need you less
O God,
than we did in the midst of
winter work and
worry.
Summer too has its sorrows,
its broken bones
and broken hearts.
The crowds in which we mingle
don't really hide our loneliness.
Our full schedules don't really
make up for the empty moments of our lives.

Be present, O God
in our play,
as well as in our prayers —
when we mow the lawn,
and when we try to make
our marriages work.

God of the Golf Course
Lord of *All* life —
This we truly pray.

Amen.

Still, sultry mornings
become stiller,
as they move toward afternoon,
with the humidity hanging
almost visible
over the heads of wrinkled and damp
passersby.
Even the children finally surrender
and move summer games indoors,
as motorists dash
from office to home
as if they were bases
in a tag game.

It's summer, God,
sticky and hot,
the way summer always is in Arkansas.
And those of us who haven't escaped
to poolside,
or lakeside,
enjoy the novelty of cable TV
in the cool isolation of our homes.

It's like a blizzard —
backwards.
We haven't seen our neighbors
in weeks,
or taken a walk
or sat on the porch,
or done anything that required
more than the barest minimum
of movement, or effort.
If it weren't for the TV, we'd be lonely —

or maybe we are lonely.

Maybe we've made
a bad trade,
exchanging cool for company —
comfort for community.

Maybe it was worth the heat
to open the windows
and hear the neighbors' voices;
the sound of fans,
and lawnmowers and laughter;
the smells
of supper
in steamy kitchens.

Maybe it was worth
the discomfort of the day
to welcome
the blue sultry cool of evening,
to lie on quilts in the grass
drinking sweaty Coca-Colas
and talking of neighbors,
and true love,
and dreams.

God,
teach us how to find each other
in our air-conditioned world
to meet,
to learn,
to share,

to let the summer be a season of
growth
and not a personal disaster
of isolation.

Amen.

God,
so very often we have called you
Father,
not because you are like our Fathers,
but because we are like children,
and calling you Father
or Mother
gives us a way of talking about
how we are related to one another
and how we feel.

It is so difficult to be known,
to be open,
and to share with one another.
It is so difficult for us
to say what we really think,
especially when it is something that
makes us vulnerable like:
"Can I help you?"
or "I care about you."

We use you as an excuse sometimes
(the way children do with their parents)
when we're afraid to admit that we're
doing the right thing — because we want to.
We say
"We come from the church,"
when what we really mean is
"We were worried about you,"
or
"I bring you this on behalf of the class"
when it would be more honest to
say "This was my idea — I wanted to
bring it."

We develop
care groups
and support systems,
phone chairmen
and outreach leaders.
We include
moments of concern in our worship
and pray intercessory prayers.

We don't really do it so much because it's Christian
as we do because we care.
We don't really do it so much because it's right
as we do because we need to support
and be supported.

We call you Father,
not because you are like our Fathers
but because we are like
brothers and sisters
here in your house.

Help us to be honest in our affections for one another,
loving each other
as you have loved us,
needing each other,
depending on each other,
bearing one another's burdens.

Amen.

God —
In the shower this morning,
that was no Angel visiting us,
it was someone wanting their
turn in the bath.

And the trumpets we heard
were not played by heavenly visitors,
unless that is the name of some new group
on the radio.

You might have tried to speak, God,
but then who could get
a word in edgewise?

Our lives are ordinary lives,
jam-packed
with ordinary cares, concerns, and chaos.
Little League
and Junior League
R.S.V.P. and U.M.Y.F.
trips to the Doctor
trips to the Dentist
trips to the Vet.

Sometimes we get bored
with the ultra-activity;
sometimes we just get tired.
Sometimes we even consider calling on you,
but feel a little foolish
asking *you* if we really need to lose five pounds.

We don't feel your presence
very often
but we know you must be around,
for if you are with those who grieve
you are with us all.
Life is such a changeful thing
that someone or something
is always growing out of our grasp.

If you are with those who are ill,
you are with us all,
for even when we're physically robust
our hearts and minds
entertain aspects of unhealth.

We don't feel your presence very often
in the shower
or in the car,
at a committee meeting
or at the pool,
but we know that you must be around
for if you are with those
who need you,
you are with us all.

Be with us — O God.

Amen.

Look at the Calendar, God.
It's July again —
July —
another birthday has happened
for everyone.
July —
and soon it will be August,
and soon we will be
ending our vacations
or going back to school,
travelling to Razorback games
or watching games on TV,
changing shorts for sweaters
and warming up the car in the cold;

but now it's July
and January's really hard to imagine,
as we water the yard,
and dash from air-conditioned house
to air-conditioned car.

That's how our lives pass us, God,
July becomes January,
and we never know
where the intervening six months went.

Kindergarten becomes College.
Brides become widows.
Spouses become strangers.
Children become parents.
Parents become children,

and then it's July again.
We reach out sometimes, God,
and try to hold
our lives still.
We touch up the gray in our hair,
and cream the wrinkles out of our face.
We play sandlot games and ignore
the pain in our knees.

We exchange glances
with younger men,
and stare at younger women.

We take photographs,
hundreds of them,
trying to freeze vignettes of our lives
to be stored for safekeeping.

But look at the Calendar, God,
or better yet
look in the mirror.
It is July again,
and today
will plunge us one day further
into the future.

God,
teach us to number our days,
not like a miser
who grasps at each coin,
but
like a parent
who values each and every child.
Teach us to welcome the birth of each morning
fresh with its unlived moments,
and to peacefully release each evening
leaving the day's fears and failures,
gains and growth
behind us,
as we slip into the death of sleep.

It is July, God,
July 20
Sunday, July 20
Give us life — this day.

Amen.

How new the world looks
this morning, God,
washed clean
by a long-awaited rain.
How new the world feels
this morning, God,
relieved from the oppressive heat
and the interminable sunshine.

And *we* seem different too,
emptied of some un-named fear,
and unconfessed helplessness.

"What's that?"
we asked each other as distinct claps of
thunder began.
"Can it be thunder?"
We threw open the doors.
Yes, it was —
it really was raining.

We opened the curtains,
and moved our conversations
to the porch.
We lingered in doorways,
and all evening long found ourselves
lured to windows just to watch.

All night we slept, lulled
by the hum of the attic fan
and the drip of the rain,

feeling safe in the world again,
unthreatened
by grim and unknown possibilities.

Dear God
we thank you,
for the recreation of the world —
for a summer rain
that can so quickly restore vitality,
for the generosity of the sky
and the wisdom of nature,
for the intricate,
infinite relationship
of Space
and Earth,
of Sun
and Sky,
of Wind
and Rain,
of Creatures
and Creator.

How new the world looks
this morning, God,
washed clean by a long-awaited rain.
How new the world feels
this morning, God,
relieved from the oppressive heat
and the interminable sunshine.

And *we* seem different too,

ready to believe again
that sorrow — like drought —
will finally dissipate,
that fear — like heat —
must eventually break,
that hope — like rain —
will surely,
always
come again.

Amen.

It's going to be
another blistering day, God,
another 105°-in-the-shade day,
where people hardly stir,
and leaves stir only
in the hot, gusty breeze.
It's too hot to work.
It's too hot to play,
and in and out of cars tempers flare,
words are short,
and the simplest kind of everyday task
becomes extraordinary labour.

Shirts are sweat-soaked,
dirty and damp and
any degree of dress
or undress
is uncomfortable.

We are uncomfortable, and we are weary
as we drag the hoses from the front yard
to the back yard,
watching the grass die,
watching the shrubs die,
watching even the leaves on the trees wither.

We are uncomfortable,
and we are powerless
because although we can save the grass
now
we can't do it indefinitely,
although we can keep cool now
we can't do that indefinitely,
and we wonder as we watch
our weekend gardens wilt
how powerless farmers must feel,
and how *we* will helplessly pay the
price of groceries next fall.

We are uncomfortable.
We are afraid because —
what if? —
What if it drags on into August
as more
trees and grass and people die.

How long can we use electricity like this?
How long can we use water like this?
We are afraid of what we can't
control — or foresee — or manage.

We are uncomfortable, and we are weary;
we are powerless, and we are afraid.

We're also a little too sophisticated
to pray for rain —
outright —
but what do we pray for
and to whom but you?
O
God of Sun and Rain —
giver of life —
earth builder,

we acknowledge
that we forget our dependence
on the simplest of natural things:
on summer sun
and seasonal rains,
on the dew of morning
and the blue-cool of twilight.

We acknowledge
that we forget our dependence
on you,
until we are humbled
by summer.

Amen.

Where has the summer gone, God?
Here it is
almost August,
and yet it seems that just yesterday
the school bells rang
to close the year in May.

Where are the years going, God?
We just rearranged the furniture,
and by the time we sat down —
I mean really sat down —
five years had passed.

The new car is not new any more;
braces have come and gone;
surgery over;
and the long-awaited trip to Europe
is now preserved forever
on Kodak slides.

Where are our lives going, God?
The hemlines have gone up and down,
and up and down,
and up again.
Ties have gotten wide,
and skinny
and wide — then skinny
then wide again,
and it seems startling
that Rosalyn is coming to Pine Bluff
because it seems that Eleanor was
the President's wife's name —
or Jackie —
or Lady something.

Sometimes
we wonder what we've spent
the summers,
the years,
our lives doing.
It all happens so quickly.

Help us
to value our lives, O God —
every summer
and every day.
Help us to capture
the invaluable individual moments
of which the fabric of life is woven.

Teach us to laugh
our laughter,
shed our tears,
recognize our anger
and cherish our tenderness.
Teach us how to love ourselves,
as you have loved us.

Amen.

Dear God,
this weekend is the last holiday
of the summer:
the last ice-cream-cone-dripping
trek to the zoo,
the last golf tournament,
the last cook-out.
The boats will now sit docked
more often than they are used,
and football will soon
take over all three channels on TV.

School has resumed,
and civic clubs
have begun their fall schedules.
Homework and dance class
begin for the chidren.

Labor Day
is in some ways
a marker that signals
"back to work,"
"back to ordinary,"
back to what has been so appropriately
termed
"the grind."

Also, God,
this week begins
the celebration of Kingdomtide.
We couldn't deny that
if we wanted to,
with splashes of green
and red and blue
inviting us to celebrate.
Crosses and plants
in vivid hues,
all symbolic of growth,
development
and change.

Kingdomtide
is in some ways
a marker that signals
"become" —
become the people of God in the world —
become the church
which can reveal his presence.

Holidays
and Holy days
come and go, O God,
marking off the rhythms of our lives,
sending us back to work,
urging us to grow and become.

We pray that our work
will become for us a way
of moving toward better lives,
as well as better lifestyles,
that we will accomplish
internal goals
as well as social achievements,

and that our worship will become
not just ritual,
but realization
as well

thy kingdom . . . tide come.

Amen.

Dear God,
as Summer moves into Autumn
and the duties
and habits
of our lives resume for another year,
we are aware
of a feeling of relief,
but relief from what?

Not from oppressive heat,
for the summer has been ~~unusually mild.~~ *fairly mild.*

Not from drought,
for the rain *pretty good*
has been ~~ample~~ this year.

Not from devastating headlines
or bizarre international events,
for, though far from peaceful,
the world is relatively quiet
these days.

And yet we feel relieved
as if the summer had been a cloud that lifted,
or a fear that dissipated.

Do we feel relieved
simply
because our schedules
are more orderly now,
because our activities
give us little time
for the difficulties
of self-evaluation
and relationship?

Or is it something larger — deeper —
that a seasonal change
touches within us
some reservoir of hope
that nature confirms —

that no situation is static
no circumstances interminable
no summer endless,
and that when our power to alter
our lives seems exhausted,
the scene changes
on its own.

The days are gradually
growing slightly shorter,
cooler;
football teams have taken the field
and Advent committees
are planning Christmas.

We are facing the future
ready to begin again,
ready to believe in ourselves again,
our marriages,
our lives,

ready to try to trust you one more time.
O Singer of Seasons,
see us through.

Amen.

God Almighty,
though we call you by many names
we acknowledge that you
are one God,
and in your eyes we are
one people

we are ordinary men and women,
come from farms and factories,
classrooms and kitchens,
to accomplish an extraordinary task.

Though we be diverse in opinion,
make us one in our commitment
to help create a more just society.

Though we be divided on issues,
unite us in our goal for a more equitable world.

Be present among us,
rich and poor,
left and right,
seekers and cynics.

May we deal with one another as graciously
as you have dealt
with us,
and although each decision
may not be right,
may it be decided rightly.

Giver of life —
This truly we pray,
each in our individual
language of faith or doubt.

Have mercy upon us, O God —
Have mercy upon us.

Arkansas Constitutional Convention
June 26, 1979

FALL

It's finally autumn, God,
the heat is finally over,
and all that remains of summer afternoons
are the closing games
between the ~~Phillies~~ and the ~~Royals~~. *Braves*

We breathe a sigh of relief
each time we open the door
upon the chilly air,
for of all hot Augusts
and dry Julys, *some of*
these were the worst
that many can remember.

We breathe a sigh of relief
as we switch the hall thermostat
from "A.C." to "Heat"
and hope that the coming winter is mild
and the bills moderate.

We breathe a sigh of relief,
for the change in the weather
is welcomed,
the thunder and the rains,
the winds that carry the brown leaves
across the yard and tease the green leaves
still on the trees,
are all welcomed signs of change yet to come.

We usually don't welcome change
God,
we usually argue
and hesitate
and balk.

We sigh —
but not with relief
when we look in the mirror to find
that passing years have left their marks
in the gray of the hair and the lines in the eyes.

We usually don't welcome change —
for the cutting down
of the tree that held our childhood playhouse,
or a construction detour
on our customary route to work,
or a different order
in the Sunday worship,
or a different hair style
becoming vogue,
reminding us that things
seldom remain the same very long,
reminding us that life is changeful,
and that our youth,
our health,
our security,
our happiness,
our relationships,
are not static
and never stand still.

Help us, O God,
as we listen
for the distant honk of autumn geese
to turn our faces
toward the unknown days of winter
to release
the joys and griefs of the past
so that our hands and hearts will be free
to embrace our coming lives.

It's finally autumn, God.

Amen.

Even if it still feels like summer,
God,
we know it's fall.
Vacations are over
and steps have quickened
to new routines.

Outside classroom windows
the marching band
souses through the sun,
while the new majorette
leads the oom pah pah
with her stumbling baton.

We know it's fall,
because football has started,
because they have put
the signs on Monroe street —
"No parking on game days" —
and the sports section
has begun to outweigh
the national news
in the daily paper.

We know it's fall
because Sunday School classes
have promoted,
sending
well rehearsed
boys and girls,
and nervous teachers
to smile at one another
shyly, as they begin a new relationship.

We know it is fall, God,
and we're glad,
for new seasons
are like doors opening
upon the yet unlived
portions of our lives.

We're glad to see
the windows of the shops change
and read the announcements
in the fashion magazines
of this year's
"New Look."

We anticipate
the nippy air — a chilly afternoon,
a frosty morning,
a brilliant splash of leaves
and football on
three channels.

We look for new faces
around corners,
expect new voices on the phones,
celebrate new relationships
and reach for new dreams.

Even though it doesn't feel like it, God,
we know it is fall,
and we see our lives
quickening,
like our pace.

For all changes, God,
and for the hope of change
we give you thanks.

Amen.

God,
we're just glad no one was taking pictures of us yesterday,
sitting in front of the TV
in our "Hog Hats."

Better still,
it's a good thing no one had a tape recorder,
to remind us later of the things we said
to the officials,
and the things we said
about the Texas band
and the Texas fans . . .

Ah, even if they had
we would probably laugh
and confess that we were as crazy as everyone else,
and that when the horn blew
and it was clear that Arkansas had won
we felt a
surge of exhilaration
and pride,
as if we personally had proven ourselves
in some fantastic contest.

"WE WON!"
We found ourselves screaming in
the street with all the neighbors,
"WE WON!"
"WE WON!"

For those who did not win,
O, God, we pray:
for the rookie who had one chance on the line,
and stepped offsides;
for the bench-sitter who never heard his number called;
for the senior who felt tendons stretch and tissues tear
and knew in a sinking moment
as he hit the ground
that a career was gone;

for those who are lonely,
for whom the raucous gaiety of the game
was a respite
from the silence of the empty house;

for those who watched
from a hospital bed,
and those who cheered
from wheelchairs;
for the avid fan
who in the wake of the death of a spouse,
or friend
found his hobby hollow,
and victory bittersweet;

for the young man
who watched on the prison lounge TV
and knew
as he watched farm boys and slum kids become heroes
that he could have;

for those who win
and for those who lose
O, God, we pray,
and we thank you for your love
that can never be lost,
for your presence
which is available to everyone,
and for your grace
which is given freely,
and which in its unconcern for merit
is the only thing that's really fair.

Amen.

The morning dawned
so clearly today, God,
that for a few moments
before the family woke
and the Sunday routine began,
life seemed very simple.

There in the quietness
of morning half-light,
with a steaming cup of coffee,
alone with our own thoughts
we understood,

that
the Cambodian peasants
who are starving by the millions
are not just staggering statistics,
but men
women and children
with names
who wake before the same sun we do.

We understood,
that the West Virginian coal miner
and the paper carrier who brought
today's *Commercial*
share with us the insecurity
of an inflationary economy.

We understood,
that the birds chattering
in the day's first light
rejoiced with us in
the undeserved beauty
of an autumn dawn.

We understood,
that beauty can't be bought,
that security has no price tag,
that the sun,
and the song of the birds,
our families' first sleepy "hellos,"
and the morning greeting
of a true friend,
are not for sale
and can't be purchased anywhere
for any kind of tender.

For a few moments
this morning, God,
life seemed that simple.
Now sitting here
amid talk of giving and balancing the
budget
we're not so sure
that anything is free.

Teach us, Gracious God,
that though
bills must be paid,
and budgets negotiated,
life is not for sale.

Teach us that giving
is an attitude,
not an act,

that the birds don't own the morning
but they exalt in it
and pass it on.

Amen.

Dear God:
We are tired of the headlines,
We are tired of the newscasts,
We are tired of angry voices,
We are tired of threats of war.

We are tired of the energy crisis,
We are tired of inflation,
We are tired of conflicting
        economic opinions,
We are tired of broken dreams.

We are tired of addressing you
        eloquently
While mobs of angry Moslems shout
        their prayers,
We are tired of the injustice
        of terrorism
Just as they are tired of being
        dominated economically,
We are tired of being hated
Just as they are tired of hating,
We are tired of being the oppressor,
We are tired of being the oppressed.

We are tired of fear,
We are tired of guilt,
We are tired of the conflictual nature
        of the world.

Dear God,
What do we do with our weariness?
Turn off the TV?
Stop reading the paper?
Blame the Moslems?
Elect a new president?

What do we do with our fear?
Turn it into military retaliation?
Suspicion?
Hate?
Prayer?

And what do we pray for —
That the Moslems' prayers will not be
    answered?
That the Ayatollah will change his mind,
And live out his faith less fervently?
What do we pray for?
Our justice?
Or theirs?

What do we pray for?

O God of all humanity,
We pray for peace,
For liberation from our fears,
For release from imprisonment
By hunger
And hate,
Self-interest
And self-satisfaction.

O Lamb of God,
We pray for mercy,
For compassion that we do not have,
For grace we do not deserve.

O Jehovah, Yahweh, Allah,
God of many names,
Single-minded Savior,
Let your people go —
Let all your people go.

Amen.

November 25, 1979
Prayed during the first weeks of the seizure
of the American Embassy in Tehran.

Some mornings, God,
it's hard to pray.

It's hard to walk up to the pulpit.
It's hard to call your name.
It's hard to gather the fears
of the week together and bless them,
and forgive them.

It's hard to sit in the pew,
to hold the hymnal,
and stifle a yawn.

It's hard to say
in confession and creed,
This is who we are:
the sleepy people
who talked too late,
and said too much,
who looked for friends
in friendly faces
and woke wondering
if our guests like us less
for having found out who we are.

This is who we are:
the angry people
who yell unfairly
at our families
about a broken rule,
or undone chore,
but know
that our impatient demands
stem from some secret anxiety
that we can't name.

This is who we are:
the broken people
who have started all over again
more than anyone will ever know,
who have salvaged our dreams
from the rubble
of grief
and fear,
and wonder
how many more punches we can roll with . . .

This is who we are:
the lonely people
who married
to guarantee ourselves
the security of at least one friend,
and yet wake some mornings to find
a stranger
in our beds,
and in our lives,
and in our mirrors.

This is who we are:
sleepy and angry
and broken
and lonely.

We find that hard to admit,
and some mornings
we find it hard to pray,
for we know you know us without
admission,
and forgive us without confession
and answer us
when we refuse to pray.

Amen.

We know them only as newspaper waifs, God,
the children of El Salvador,
and the widows,
who turn their wailing faces camera-ward
and unknowingly
share their grief with distant millions
who are munching pizza
and arguing about the car keys,
with Walter Cronkite's voice in the background.

And the children of Greece
who wander through the rubble of their towns
looking for the particular
pile of rubble that was their home.

We know them only as interviewees,
the unemployed workers of Detroit
who stop as they pass the plant gate
to tell a microphone
in their strange northern accent
that they have no plans,
they don't know what they'll do.

We know the frightened black faces of Atlanta
as well as we know
the gaunt but happy faces of returning hostages.

We've seen Polish strikers smiling
and Russian officials sternly staring.
We've seen Prince Charles
introduce his bride,
and Brezhnev falter with age
and weariness in his speech.

We have seen the faces of the
world in our kitchens and our dens
and heard their pain or joy
blurted out for all to hear.

We have seen ambulances dash across the screen
and watched excited reporters
call out the details
of fire,
and fear,
and death.

We have seen and we have heard
but we did not stop washing the supper potatoes;
we did not
lay down the sports report.

We did not
lay down the fork for a moment
in sorrow or disbelief.

We did not call your name
or ask why
or plead for some release from
that far-away pain.

We did not — for we have grown jaded,
for the 6:00 horror
is followed by the 10:00 horror,
or the printed horror of the morning paper.
For the crack of a real gun in El Salvador
is juxtaposed with
fictional guns of late night Gunsmoke;
the distress of a wailing widow
fades into the commercial distress
of a housewife
over the price of peanut butter.

Forgive us, O God,
for our eyes that no longer see,
ears that no longer hear,
hearts that no longer pray.

We pray.

Amen.

Whenever they talk about money
we usually tune
the thing out —
or when they ask for volunteers
to give time
to some project,
we stop listening
and the scene is like
TV with the sound turned down.

We're not miserly,
or uninvolved,
at least not any more than anyone else —
But we're overextended,
tired, stretched thin.

The income
doesn't seem to cover the outlay —
whether it's cash flow
or time,
energy or tears

and though we've moved into a house
that solidifies our social position
and seem to be doing so well —
dressed well,
all smiles,
we know in many ways we're poverty stricken —
short on cash,
short on love,
short on peace.
God,
we don't know how to give
when the stuff of life is so scarce.

Give us, O God,
a good night's sleep,
a quiet moment in the middle of the day,
a day without pain,
an unexpected phone call,
a memory,
a smile,
the peace of self-appreciation,
the solid song of someone else's love,
a hot bath,
a kind word from a stranger,
our favorite song ten years ago
played on the radio,
a surprise birthday party,
tenderness from our spouse,
authenticity from our children,
cooperation from our parents.
Give us cool days so the electric
bills won't soar,
and cool nights
so we can sleep.

Give us the ability
to give
to have confidence in our lives
that a gift
of love
or time
or money
won't break the bank.
Give us your presence,
O Giver —
Give us life.

Amen.

Almighty God,
we've worked hard this week,
maybe too hard,
because in our weariness it seems as if
everyone is calling our name:
our family,
our friends,
our colleagues
all have claims upon us,
and our time and energies all seem to belong
to someone else.

Even here,
where we hope to hear about *grace*,
and God's gifts to us,
we confront again the questions of obligation
and commitment.

Time, money, loyalty —
There just doesn't seem to be enough to go around.
We sometimes think that's because
we're not as capable as others,
and we begin to feel bad about ourselves,
and we try to cover that up by working harder
and getting tireder.

Time, money, loyalty —
There just doesn't seem to be enough to go around.
We sometimes think that's because
you've treated us unfairly,
by giving others more,
and we begin to grow angry with you
and resentful of others.

God,
we know that these are inadequate understandings,
but we don't really know
what the alternatives are.
We don't know how to take the gifts
we have received
and share them with one another
without emptying ourselves;
to give time to someone
without feeling rushed the rest of the day;
to give of ourselves without feeling insecure
and defenseless;
to give money without thinking of all the things
we always wanted.

Help us to understand the dynamics of commitment;
to learn how to receive
from what we give;
to learn how to sing as we work
and to be honest about our limits,
and confident of your limitless concern
and gracious giving of life.

Help us to listen to your advice
about how we should manage our lives,
not like businesses,
shrewdly considering investments and returns,
but like wildflowers
who by simply being themselves
share a beauty that surpasses
humanity's most artistic labors.

Help us to know that what we are is enough,
that what we have is enough,

and that it is you who will replenish
our strength
and restore our spirits
when we have emptied ourselves
for others.

Amen.

God,
we are people who have traveled to *this* place
today
from various places in separate yesterdays,
and we have memories of our lives that are past.
Sometimes those memories are good,
and sometimes they are not so good.

It is good to be able to remember,
and you yourself
remind us who we are by confronting us
with your word,
and with the symbols of the history of our
relationship with you.

But sometimes we keep those memories like trophies
that make us proud.
Sometimes we keep those memories like scars
that make us despair.

Trophies and scars are both very heavy
to carry with one for very long.
And that's why we've come here,
because we're tired —
    tired of trying to live up to the past,
    or tired of trying to live the past down.

We want to be in your presence,
where the past is accepted
and each moment becomes a new opportunity
to be who we are.

We want to be with one another in your presence,
and see each other
through your eyes . . . and accept one another
in this moment
without the cumbersome grudges
and misunderstandings of the past.

We want this,
and this is why we've come
but even now we will try to hide from you
and from each other
because we're afraid of ourselves
and of the risk of starting all over again
and again.

The words of our worship become something
with which we are familiar and comfortable,
but we're still uncomfortable after all these years,
with these feelings of need
and we would rather cling to the old familiar
ghosts of hurt feelings and disappointed
expectations than open ourselves to the unknown.

God,
we will try to forgive ourselves;
we will forgive one another
and we'll make a habit of remembering to forget.

Help us
as we reach for a commitment to the present
and a vision of the future
in your promise of freedom from the past.

Amen.

Just an ordinary Autumn
would have been okay, God,
just an ordinary Autumn of muted browns,
with an occasional splash of gold.

After the heat of the Summer
we would have been happy
with a quiet,
unspectacular change of the season —
in fact
that's really what we were prepared for.

We were not prepared
for this Autumn,
or for the spell that you
have cast over the world.

Red, gold, green, brown
and every shade between
continue to surprise us,
for the contrast becomes
more brilliant
each day —
when we didn't think it could.

We dawdle at our desks,
gazing out the window
in a trance
of unbelief.
We create errands to run,
find reasons
to walk or drive outside.
We pry open windows,
long painted shut,
fearful that the enchantment
will soon be over
and the world will be itself again.

Each day
we evaluate with our neighbors;
we say,
"I think it has just about peaked,"
and yet the next day
is more beautiful still.

It can't last much longer,
we know that
temperatures will drop,
and so must leaves.
We know it can't last much longer
and that is a part
of its breath-taking power —
that it is so briefly wonderful,
it will not be taken for granted.

Teach us, O God,
to respect the brief beauty
of our lives like that:
to value a baby's cry
for it will soon change:
to treasure one another's laughter
in its momentary unison:
to wake and for a moment pause
to marvel lovingly at a sleeping spouse:

to bless our ordinary joys
and brief happinesses
as they pass.

Just an ordinary Autumn
would have been okay, God,
but for this one we give you thanks.

Amen.

We have come here
out of habit, God,
because we always have,
because —
well, that's just Sunday:
the alarm,
the comics,
a shower,
the search for a missing shoe,
Sunday School,
Church,
the Pot Roast at lunch,
a nap,
sports on TV.
Week after week,
year after year,
Sunday comes and we come here.

We know that there are other reasons
for coming to church.
We teach them to the children
in Sunday School,
but to be perfectly honest,
the times
that we have made the drive
thinking of worship — and an encounter
with the "holy" —
are just too few to talk about.

We come
for someone to talk to,
for the ten minutes of coffee
and chatter
before Sunday School,
where we can mention casually
the fears
and insecurities
that have nagged our weeknight sleep.

We come,
hoping someone else
feels the way we feel,
and asks the same questions,
so that during a discussion
we don't feel
alone
and disapproved of.

We come,
because after a week of waving,
as we pass our spouse in the driveway,
or meeting the kids briefly
at the refrigerator,
we welcome the opportunity
to go one place — at one time — together.

We come
because the preacher's good,
because
even though sometimes we haven't
heard of the book of the Bible
he reads from,
he usually says something
that comforts us,
or challenges us,
or makes us think.

We come because our friends do,
or the boss does;
because it's good business,
or good politics.
We come for many reasons,
most of which we'd never admit.

And although
they aren't pious reasons,
or holy reasons,
or ideal reasons,
they have one thing
that recommends them —
they have brought us
into your presence.

Blessed is the habit
that brings us again and again to you.

Blessed is the habit
that causes us again and again to
pray.

Amen.

WINTER

Dear God,

We did not want to come this morning.
We did not want to get out of bed.

When we woke to the sound of leaves
charging around the house
in the wind,
and caught a glimpse of wintery sky
through the parted curtain,
we wanted to roll over
and settle into the warmth of our pillows
for awhile,
or follow the lure
of a smoking cup of coffee
to the fireplace,
and the newspaper.

"No one would miss us anyway,"
we told ourselves.
"We can sit right here
and watch the service on TV,
and it will be all the same."

That sounded good,
and we believed it for awhile,
until we caught another glimpse of sky.
It was the lonely gray of winter,
and it struck a painful chord within us.
It reminded us of something.

Oh, not an event or occurrence
we can remember,
but a feeling we can never forget.

It reminded us
of how lonely we feel sometimes,
how chilly and empty.

It reminded us that in elevators
we worry about dying —
when we're X-rayed
we wonder "What if" —
at funerals
we squelch our angry cry of "Why?"

It reminded us
of the times when the children
were late from the school bus,
and we *helplessly* paced;
or the times we arrived home
from work
and no one was there.

The black bare branches against the sky
reminded us of mornings in the mirror
when we see
the once lovely faces of our youth becoming
catalogues
of anxiety for all to see.

The chilly gusts
of leaves nipping at the house
reminded us
of the terrible flights of our fantasy
when we hear a noise in the night.

This morning,
standing in the various kitchens
and corridors of our lives,
we felt the fullness of our frailty
and we came here

for the reassurance
that others too are afraid,
and to hear the good news,
the word that we are not alone.

Oh God of Winter starkness
and Summer joys,
we have come to sing
and to dance,
to feel the warmth of human comfort,
and the awesomeness of Divine presence.
Here we are.
Love us.

Amen.

The bustle has begun, God,
the month-long
mad dash through shopping centers
and stores
has started,

and even though we swore
last year
that we would never do *that* again,
that we would never spend
our evenings and week-ends
elbowing through crowds,
or wandering around
a parking lot looking for our car,
or running up a Mastercard bill
that will take a year to pay,

we have become a part of it again.

As we put the last stamp on
the last envelope
last year,
we promised ourselves —
"No more Christmas cards."

And yet this year
we couldn't resist
the temptation to send — "just a few" —
a list that has grown
until it's longer than ever before.

We are a part of it all, God,
all of the tinsel,
all of the gaudiness,
all of the brazen commercial
      "Ho, Ho, Ho."
We can't sit on the sidelines
and philosophize
that Christmas has become too secular,
that the real meaning has been
buried in bows and wrapping.
We can't criticize
the way our society celebrates,
because we are our society.

When the Symphony Designer House
opened,
we were there.

At the pre-Christmas decoration sales
we were there.
We pass each other in the shops
and chat at the nursery
as we buy our trees,
and on Christmas Eve,
when the last hearty shoppers
race the clock to the store,
we will remember
at least
two gifts
we have to have.

No, we can't philosophize
for we confess
if Santa has helpers —
they are us!
We can't criticize,
for if Christ has been forgotten
at Christmas
we're the ones who forgot.

We can ask this, O God,
we *can* ask
that if our celebrations are hollow
you fill them with your presence,
transform our shopping list
from a checklist of obligations
to a real rejoicing
in those we love.
Turn traditions
into togetherness,
and may the presents we open
this year
truly be gifts.

Enter our hearts once more —
and startle us in the parking lots
of our own lives
as you did
the innkeepers
and shopkeepers
of another day.

Teach us to celebrate,
to dance
and to love.

Amen.

God,
we've overdone it again!
We didn't mean to — we thought we were being
sensible this year.
It didn't seem like there were *that* many gifts
under the tree,
until the wrappings just filled the room;

The ham didn't really seem *that* big
until we couldn't get it in the pan.

We thought we had been prudent and turned
down so many good things to eat,
until we stepped on the scales.

It's true, we got all caught up once again,
in the hassle and the hurry and the "Ho, Ho, Ho."
We spent all of our money
and then some
on all kinds of things
that we don't really need.

We've had such a good time,
we've plotted and planned and played
like children.

And now like children who've gotten into the cookie jar,
we're beginning to anticipate getting caught.
We're beginning to feel a little silly,
and we know that soon we'll feel guilty.

Our serious selves will look around
at the aftermath of affluence
and say,
"Maybe we missed the true message of Christmas."

But, God,
It's such a grim world sometimes.
There seem to be so few things to really celebrate
and we seldom go all out
to say, "I love you."

The World Hunger posters are still
hanging in the hallway there.
We're not trying to excuse ourselves
from our responsibilities,
but we know that it is true, as Judy Collins sang,
"Hearts starve as well as bodies."

As we look at ourselves
this Christmas Day,
we really surprise ourselves
because
you know for all our grumbles and gripes,
for all our skepticism,
we really do believe in you — in each other
and in ourselves.

We really can forget unpleasant incidents
and harsh words,
we really can forgive pain, betrayal
and disappointment.

We really can
not only talk about peace,
but in our childlike joy
forget our fears
and really share the gift of peace with
one another.

Maybe — we haven't missed the message after all.

Happy Birthday, Jesus —
and thank you.

Amen.

Dear God,
we are aware
of the excess of it all;
we are aware
that we spend too much,
eat too much,
worry too much.

We know that we overextend the bank accounts,
and the calorie counts,
that we stay up too late
and plan more than we can
possibly do.

We R.S.V.P. "Yes"
to too many parties,
too many meals,
too many gifts,
too many cards,
too many guests,
too much celebration. . .

until New Year's Day
begins to seem
like the long-awaited end
of a self-imposed seige.

We are aware of the excess of it all
and we complain to one another
in the aisles of the shopping mall
or as we wait in line at the 24-hour bank.

We grumble when we look at price tags,
gasp when the cashier rings the total,
and we anticipate that we'll complain afresh
each month when the Visa bill arrives.

We didn't set out to have a harried holiday —
we really didn't.
In fact each year
we resolve
to have a quieter, slower
December,
a more sensible Christmas.

It just never happens that way.

Dear God,
in this quiet moment
in this still house
as we sit perfectly silent,
stifling a cough,

grant us a moment's peace.

As we shuffle our feet
and look at our watch
and wonder if the TV cameras
have shut off yet,

grant us a moment's joy.

As we worry about
the noises we can hear coming
from the nursery
and wish the man next to us
would stop sneezing,

grant us a moment's love.

In the name of the Christ-child,
the Christmas baby —

Amen.

Dear God,
We would like to pretend
that what happens here
is of no consequence to us.

We would like to pretend
that we are nonchalant
about this gathering.

We've been accused
so often
of being here for social reasons,
or to make business contacts,
or just because it's a habit.
We almost wish those accusations
were true.

The truth is more painful than that.
The truth is,
we have something invested here.

The truth is,
we are intrigued by
the possibility that there is hope;
that there can be peace;
that people can care for one another;
that someone cares for us.

We need to be cared for;
we need
to see some kind of sense
of order in life.

We need to discover the purposes
of things.
We need to affirm a meaning
for our actions and our existence.

We're here because we need,
and we're taking the chance
that here our needs will be understood
and maybe

just maybe
all this talk of God
and power,
of Grace
and guidance
is not just talk.

Maybe we're not just stumbling
along blindly — selfishly —
fatally —
Maybe what we do really does matter.
Maybe we are worthwhile.

"Maybe" is why we came,
and we're not nonchalant
about the outcome.

Forgive us for our doubts,
O God,
and give us the courage
to continue to say "Yes"
to the challenge of faith.

Yes, God,
we do care.

Amen.

Lord, look at us —
so still, so quiet,
so contemplative.

You know
we're not nearly as quiet
as we seem.

You know we're on the run:
running from facts,
and fantasies,
and fears;
running from the mirror,
and running from you,
because you know
what we manage to conceal
beneath a smile
and a stylish suit of clothes.

We've got problems.
Oh, we don't want to get dramatic.
We certainly don't want sympathy,

but there are things
we worry about alone,
that no one else really knows:

the bank balance,
the kids,
the taxes,
the job,
those nagging headaches.

Sometimes you know
we find ourselves wishing
that everything would just crash in
on us.
Then we would be through with it,
and we could start all over,
but you can't start all over
if things never end,
can you?

What a relief it would be
to declare emotional bankruptcy,
and feel forgiven
and free from old fears.

But instead, we decide,
that there's no need to get the family worried;
after all
we can surely work something out.

We want to be honest with you,
but then we confess
you are too often a parent figure
to us.
We want to please you.
We want you to be proud of us
more than we want you to know us.

Teach us how to be ourselves,
to look in the mirror and see
both joys and pains,
problems and pleasures.

Teach us how to share our burdens
with you and with one another.

Teach us, O God most holy
to rejoice in being human,
broken but beautiful, fallen but free.

In the name of the one
who became human with us
in order that he might be
God for us —

Amen.

God,
it wasn't the casserole
that kept us awake last night,
although there was too much seasoning,
and we did eat too much.

No,
it was another kind of heartburn
that kept us up,
made us toss and turn
and lie staring at the ceiling
in the dark.

It was *that* feeling again;
the one where you want something,
but you don't know what;
you want to go,
but you don't know where;
you want something to happen,
but nothing seems to be the right thing.

It's the feeling that, when we were children,
made us get into fights at school,
and when we were older,
cruise down Cherry Street
with a carload of our friends
looking for something.

Now we just work harder,
or argue with the boss,
or our husbands,
or our wives,
or cry in the middle of the day,
or go hunting
and shoot at everything.

If it gets really bad,
we buy a new dress
or a new car,
and that helps — for a while.

I guess for more than any other reason,
that's why we're here.
We feel restless and we're looking for something.

We would like to have
this feeling over with
once and for all.

You know, I guess at times like this
we really understand how
some other people worship.

It really would feel good to be
loud and honest,
and get struck down by the Spirit
in some undeniable way.

Maybe that kind of high
wouldn't last,
but it would feel good
for a while —
like a new car.

God, we're searching for you,
and for ourselves,
for a way to live
and to keep living.

If we knew how to find
we would have found already.
If we knew a formula or a phrase
that would conjure you up,
we would have used it long ago.
In fact, we tried a few.

God, we feel empty and restless and human
and discouraged and afraid.
Maybe we feel silly saying that, now,
in the morning light.

We really shouldn't feel like that;
everything seems
to be O.K.

But it kept us awake —
It has before;
it probably will again.

Come to us, Almighty God,
Grant us reassurance,
the stillness of your spirit,
and the security of your love.

Be what we are looking for.
Be where we are going.
Be with us when we can't sleep.

Amen.

What a surprise it was,
God,
to wake this morning
and find the snow.
What a surprise
to expect a gray winter day
or, at best,
another blue and brown day,
and open the curtains instead
on a world of white.

What a surprise it was, God,
and something inside us
made us feel like children —
delighted,
excited,
in love with a world that can change
overnight.
But we're not children, God.
We know the world *is*
the world in which we went to sleep
last night.

We know that some
have difficulty heating their homes,
or paying the bills,
or keeping a job,
or coping with their lives.

Some watched the snow fall
through the window of a cell,
or over the ruins of a marriage,
or from a hospital waiting room.

We know the world hasn't changed
overnight, God,
but thank you for the white reminder
that the unexpected
is always waiting in the wings.
Thank you
for helping us feel like children again —
welcoming the unpredictable,
ready to delight
and dream.

Thank you for tapping us on the shoulder —
so to speak —
to tell us you're still in charge,
and as long as you are
we will be at least halfway ready
to find unforecasted snow,
or an angel in the road,
or a dream come to life.

What a surprise it was, God,
To wake and find the snow.
Thank you.

Amen.

Almighty God,
we've cleaned our houses this week,
and tried to get the offices in shape
for another year of business as usual.

Everything it seems has finally settled down
after the holidays.

Children are back in school
and familiar routines are returning.

We didn't realize,
until we were mounting this year's holiday photos
with pictures of holidays past,
how much we've changed,
how different we are —
not that anyone else would notice.

In fact, it's been so gradual
we've hardly noticed it ourselves.
But we've come a long way
on our journeys.

Oh, the stars we've picked to follow
weren't always the right ones,
and we've taken more than a few
wrong turns,
followed the wrong signs
or sometimes just our noses.

Our dreams and our directions
have changed
and changed again.

Goals, deadlines and destinations
have been shuffled,
re-evaluated and exchanged.

We've stumbled and sprinted,
turned back,
then turned to start again.

Maybe we're surprised
when we look at ourselves,
because we never expected to make it this far,
or maybe we're amazed
that no matter how far off-course our searches were,
you always seemed to find us.

For all our pomp,
we are just pilgrims;
and though we compete in "mapmaking"
and have a lot of advice for each other
about the proper courses to take,
we are lost most of the time,
not knowing exactly where we are,
or exactly where it is we're going.

Forgive us
for loving our security more than your goals,
and our certainty
more than the risk necessary to follow you.

We've come a long way,
and we've been neither wise
nor faithful.

We are going,
we are growing.

Travel with us, Lord,
so that our roads, however crooked,
may end with you.

Amen.

We should feel great
this morning, God —
Everything adds up to exuberance.

A beautiful crisp coming of
dawn,
the promise of a perfect
afternoon,
the prospect of another night
crowded with stars —
balmy, brooding,
moving toward spring.

We should feel great, for
Eric Heiden won five
gold medals
and the U.S. Hockey team
surprised everyone,
especially the Russians.

The flu is almost over
and hayfever
is not yet here —
The hurry of the New Year has passed
and the hectic dash to the lake
has not begun.

The world seems calmer,
the threat of war
not quite as imminent
the talk of armament
not quite as adamant.

We should feel great,
and yet,
we got out of bed
reluctantly —
we dawdled.
We didn't speak sharply —
not on this beautiful day —
but we could have.

We should feel great,
and yet,
there is some unspoken tension,
some unfaced fear,
some unclaimed anxiety
that burdens us —
quiets us —
like the solemn purple of Lent.

Is it because we know
that this is a sudden world
in which well-being
is often tentative.
Is it because we know
that February gives no
guarantee of good weather.

Is it because we know
the sorrow of Lent
precedes the joy of Easter.

Is it because
behind Heiden
and the flamboyant fulfillment of his
dream,
there skated young men whose
hopes slowly dissolved
in defeat — and anonymity.

We should feel great
this morning, God, and we are
as exuberant as cautious
reality will let us be.
Help us bear the beauty of this life, O God,
and to not be afraid of
February-Spring.

Help us to laugh even when
we know tears are not far away,
to celebrate victories — even
if they are not ours,

and to befriend
this most uncertain world.

February 1980 — the week of Eric Heiden's
1980 Olympic gold medal for skating.

God,
we've turned up our thermostats again,
and shoveled our sidewalks — three times.
We feel sort of helpless,
the bad weather just keeps on coming,
and the snow that was a novelty
two weeks ago
is beginning to try our patience.

We're in control most of the time,
you know,
and when something like this winter
comes along,
we get frustrated —

frustrated enough to begin to understand
how it feels to have external
conditions control us,
how some people
are the everyday victims
and casualties
of weather,
and wind,
and birth,
and politics.

Help us, God,
not to forget — when our skies
become sunny again,
and we become mobile
and routinely on top of things —
that some people never are
in charge of their lives.

They're not just unknown third-world people,
but people in our own midst
who need our help
and our company,
not our sympathy
but our acknowledgement that we
are all rained upon
or snowed upon
by the same storms.

Help us to admit our limits
and our fears.

Amen.